THE PRACTICAL STRATEGIES SERIES
IN GIFTED EDUCATION

series editors

FRANCES A. KARNES & KRISTEN R. STEPHENS

Curriculum Compacting
An Easy Start to Differentiating
for High-Potential Students

Sally M. Reis & Joseph S. Renzulli

PRUFROCK PRESS, INC.

At the time of this book's publication, all facts and figures cited are the most current available. All telephone numbers, addresses, and Web site URLs are accurate and active. All publications, organizations, Web sites, and other resources exist as described in the book, and all have been verified. The authors and Prufrock Press, Inc., make no warranty or guarantee concerning the information and materials given out by organizations or content found at Web sites, and we are not responsible for any changes that occur after this book's publication. If you find an error, please contact Prufrock Press, Inc. We strongly recommend to parents, teachers, and other adults that you monitor children's use of the Internet.

Prufrock Press, Inc.
P.O. Box 8813
Waco, Texas 76714-8813
(800) 998-2208
Fax (800) 240-0333
http://www.prufrock.com

Contents

The Practical Strategies Series in Gifted Education offers teachers, counselors, administrators, parents, and other interested parties with up-to-date instructional techniques and information on a variety of issues pertinent to the field of gifted education. Each guide addresses a focused topic and is written by scholars with authority on the issue. Several guides have been published. Among the titles are:

- *Acceleration Strategies for Teaching Gifted Learners*
- *Curriculum Compacting: An Easy Start to Differentiating for High-Potential Students*
- *Enrichment Opportunities for Gifted Learners*
- *Independent Study for Gifted Learners*
- *Motivating Gifted Students*
- *Questioning Strategies for Teaching the Gifted*
- *Social & Emotional Teaching Strategies*
- *Using Media & Technology With Gifted Learners*

For a current listing of available guides within the series, please contact Prufrock Press at (800) 998-2208 or visit http://www.prufrock.com.

In order to accommodate for the needs of students across so many different levels of academic achievement, many teachers have adopted a variety of within-classroom strategies collectively referred to as "differentiated instruction." Differentiation is an attempt to address the variation of learners in the classroom through multiple approaches that modify instruction and curricula to match the individual needs of students (Tomlinson, 2000). Tomlinson (1995) emphasized that, when teachers differentiate the curriculum, they stop acting as dispensers of knowledge and instead serve as organizers of learning opportunities. Differentiation of instruction and curricula suggests that students can be provided with materials and work of varied levels of difficulty with scaffolding, diverse kinds of grouping, and different time schedules (Tomlinson, 2000).

Renzulli (1977a, 1988; Renzulli & Reis, 1997) defined differentiation as encompassing five dimensions: content, process, products, classroom organization and management, and the teacher's commitment to change him- or herself into a learner, as well as a teacher. The differentiation of *content* involves adding more depth to the curriculum by focusing on structures of knowledge, basic principles, functional concepts, and methods of inquiry in particular disciplines. The differentiation of *process* incorporates the use of various instructional strategies and materials to enhance and motivate various students' learning styles. The differentiation of *products* enhances students' communication skills by encouraging them to express themselves in a variety of ways. To differentiate *classroom management*, teachers can change the physical environment and grouping patterns they use in class and vary the allocation of time and resources for both groups and individuals. Classroom differentiation strategies can also be greatly enhanced by using the Internet in a variety of creative ways. Last, teachers can differentiate *themselves* by modeling the roles of athletic or drama coaches, stage or production managers, promotional agents, and academic advisers. All these roles differ qualitatively from the role of teacher-as-instructor. Teachers can also "inject" themselves into the material through artistic modification (Renzulli, 1988), a process that guides teachers in the sharing of direct, indirect, and vicarious experiences related to personal interests, travel experiences, collections, hobbies, and other extracurricular involvements that can enhance content.

Curriculum compacting is a differentiation strategy that incorporates content, process, products, classroom management, and the teacher's personal commitment to accommodating individual and small-group differences. This approach can benefit teachers of all grades in most content areas, and it addresses the demand for more challenging learning experiences designed to help all students achieve at high levels and realize their potential.

Curriculum Compacting:
Definitions and Steps for Implementation

Curriculum compacting streamlines the grade-level curriculum for high potential students to enable time for more challenging and interesting work. This differentiation strategy was specifically designed to make appropriate curricular adjustments for students in any curricular area and at any grade level. The procedure involves (1) defining the goals and outcomes of a particular unit or block of instruction; (2) determining and documenting the students who have already mastered most or all of a specified set of learning outcomes; and (3) providing replacement strategies for material already mastered through the use of instructional options that enable a more challenging, interesting, and productive use of the student's time.

Most teachers indicate that they are committed to meeting students' individual needs. Yet, many teachers do not have background information to put this commitment into practice. Research has demonstrated that many talented students receive little differentiation of curriculum and instruction and spend a great deal of time in school doing work they have already mastered (Archambault et al., 1993; Reis et al., 1993; Westberg, Archambault, Dobyns, & Salvin 1993). Too often, for example, some of our brightest students spend time relearning material they already know, which can lead to frustration, boredom, and, ultimately, underachievement. Curriculum compacting has been effective in addressing underachievement when the compacted regular curriculum is replaced with self-selected work in a high interest area, making schoolwork much more enjoyable (Baum, Renzulli & Hébert, 1995; Reis et al.).

Most teachers who use compacting learn to streamline the curriculum through a practical, step-by-step approach to the skills required to modify curricula and the techniques for pretesting students and preparing enrichment and acceleration options based on individual areas of interest. Practical issues such as record keeping and how to use the compacting form are also necessary to help guide teachers toward implementing this strategy. Once they have tried to compact for students, these guidelines can help save valuable classroom time for both teachers and students.

Curriculum compacting has been field tested since 1975. It has been used with individuals and groups of students with above-average ability in virtually every academic, artistic, or vocational area. Most important, research demonstrates that compacting can dramatically reduce redundancy and challenge gifted students to new heights of excellence (Reis et al., 1993). It can be particularly meaningful for high-ability students who are underachieving because it provides one clear way to streamline work that may be too easy and replace it with more challenging work and also with self-selected opportunities in that area or in another area of interest.

Many educators would like to adapt the regular curriculum for their above-average students. Accomplishing this, however, is no small task. Too little time, too many curricular objectives, and poor organizational structures can all take their toll on even the most dedicated professionals. This publication is designed to help teachers overcome those obstacles. Targeted for elementary and middle-level educators, it explains how to stream-line, or "compact," the curriculum through a practical, step-by-step approach. Readers will learn the skills required to modify the curriculum, as well as techniques for pretesting students and preparing enrichment options. Practical issues such as record keeping and administrative support are also included. Both efficient and complete, these guidelines will save valuable classroom time for both teachers and students.

An overview of the curriculum compacting process is best provided by the use of the management form "The Compactor," as presented in Figure 1. It serves as both an organizational and record-keeping tool. Teachers usually complete one form per student or one form for a group of students with similar curricular strengths. Completed Compactors should be kept in students' academic files and updated regularly. The form can also be used for small groups of students who are working at approximately the same level (e.g., a reading or math group) and as an addendum to an Individualized Education Plan (IEP).

The Compactor is divided into three columns:

1. The first column includes information on learning objectives and student strengths in those areas. Teachers should list the objectives for a particular unit of study, followed by data on students' proficiency in those objectives, including test scores, behavioral profiles, and past academic records.

INDIVIDUAL EDUCATIONAL PROGRAMMING GUIDE

The Compactor

Prepared by: Joseph S Renzulli
Linda H. Smith

NAME

SCHOOL

AGE

GRADE

TEACHER(S)

PARENT(S)

Individual Conference Dates And Persons Participating In Planning Of IEP

CURRICULUM AREAS TO BE CONSIDERED FOR COMPACTING   Provide a brief description of basic material to be covered during this marking period and the assessment information or evidence that suggests the need for compacting.

PROCEDURES FOR COMPACTING BASIC MATERIAL   Describe activities that will be used to guarantee proficiency in basic curricular areas.

ACCELERATION AND/OR ENRICHMENT ACTIVITIES   Describe activities that will be used to provide advanced level learning experiences in each area of the regular curriculum.

☐ Check here if additional information is recorded on the reverse side

Copyright © 1978 by Creative Learning Press, Inc. PO Box 320 Mansfield Center, Ct. 06250. All rights reserved.

Figure 1. The compactor

Note. From *The Compactor* (pp. 77–78), by J. S. Renzulli and L. H. Smith, 1978, Mansfield Center, CT: Creative Learning Press. Copyright ©1978 by Creative Learning Press. Reprinted with permission.

2. In the second column, teachers should list the ways in which they will preassess whether students already know the skills that will be taught in class. The pretest or preassessment strategies they select, along with results of those assessments, should be listed in this column. The assessment instruments can be formal measures, such as tests, or informal measures, such as performance assessments based on observations of class participation and written assignments. Specificity of knowledge and objectives is important; recording an overall score of 85% on 10 objectives, for example, sheds little light on what portion of the material can be compacted, since students might show limited mastery of some objectives and complete mastery of others.

3. The third column is used to record information about acceleration or enrichment options. To determine these options, teachers must consider students' individual interests and learning styles. They should not uniformly replace compacted regular curriculum work with harder, more advanced material that is determined solely by the teacher. Many years of research and field testing have determined that, when teachers do this, students will learn a major lesson: if they do their best work, they are rewarded with more and harder work. Instead, we recommend that students' interests be considered. If, for example, a student enjoys working on science fair projects, time to work on these projects can be used to replace material already mastered in a different content area. Teachers should be careful to monitor the challenge level of the material being substituted. Too often, talented students do not understand the nature of effort and challenge because everything they encounter in school is too easy for them. Teachers must attempt to replace the compacted material with work that is engaging and challenging.

How to Use the Compacting Process

Defining Goal and Outcomes

The first of three phases of the compacting process consists of defining the goals and outcomes of a given unit or segment of instruction. This information is readily available in most subjects because specific goals and outcomes are included in teachers' manuals, curriculum guides, scope-and-sequence charts, and some of the new curricular frameworks that are emerging in connection with outcome-based education models. Teachers should examine these objectives to determine which represent the acquisition of new content or thinking skills as opposed to reviews or practice of material that has previously been taught. The scope-and-sequence charts prepared by publishers or a simple comparison of the table of contents of a basal series will provide a quick overview of new versus repeated material. A major goal of this phase of the compacting process is to help teachers make individual programming decisions; a larger professional development goal is to help teachers be better analysts of the material they are taught and better consumers of textbooks and prescribed curricular materials.

Identifying Students

The second phase of curriculum compacting is to identify students who have already mastered the objectives or outcomes of a unit or segment of instruction that is about to be taught. Many of these students have the potential to master new material at a faster than normal pace; and, of course, knowing one's students well is the best way to begin the assessment process. Standardized achievement tests can serve as a good general screen for this step because they allow teachers to list the names of all students who are scoring one or more years above grade level in particular subject areas.

Being a candidate for compacting does not necessarily mean that a student knows all of the material under consideration. Therefore, the second step in identifying candidates involves the use of assessment techniques to evaluate specific learning outcomes. Unit pretests or end-of-unit tests that can be given as pretests are appropriate for this task, especially when it comes to the assessment of basic skills. An analysis of pretest results enables the teacher to document proficiency in specific skills and to select instructional activities or practice material necessary to bring the student up to a high level on any skill that may need some additional reinforcement.

The process is slightly modified for compacting content areas that are not as easily assessed as basic skills and for students who have not mastered the material, but are judged to be candidates for more rapid coverage. First, students should understand the goals and procedures of compacting, including the nature of the replacement process. Underachieving students often regard compacting as a bargain, as they may be able to compact out of a segment of material they already know (e.g., a unit that includes a series of chapters in a social studies text). The procedures for verifying mastery at a high level should be specified. These procedures might consist of answering questions based on the chapters, writing an essay, or taking the standard end-of-unit test. The amount of time for completion of the unit should be specified, and procedures such as periodic progress reports or log entries for teacher review should be discussed and selected.

Providing Acceleration and Enrichment Options

The final phase of the compacting process can be one of the most exciting aspects of teaching because it is based on cooperative decision making and creativity on the parts of both teachers and students. Time saved through curriculum compacting can be used to provide a variety of enrichment and acceleration opportunities for the student.

Enrichment strategies might include those found in the Enrichment Triad Model (Renzulli, 1977a), which provide opportunities for exposure to new topics and ideas, creative and critical thinking activities, and opportunities to pursue advanced independent or small-group creative projects. This aspect of the compacting process should also be viewed as a creative opportunity for a teacher to serve as a mentor to one or two students who are not working up to their potential. There is another interesting occurrence that has resulted from the availability of curriculum compacting: When some previously bright, but underachieving students realize they can both economize on regularly assigned material and "earn time" to pursue self-selected interests, their motivation to complete regular assignments increases. As one student put it, "Everyone understands a good deal!"

Several strategies have been suggested for differentiating instruction and curricula for talented or high-potential students. They range from substitution of regular material for more advanced material, to options such as independent program or specific-content strategies (e.g., Great Books or Literature Circles). Many of these strategies can be used in combination with compacting or as replacement ideas after the students' curriculum has been compacted, as can acceleration, which enables students to engage in content that is appropriately challenging (Southern & Jones, 1992; Stanley, 1989) by joining students in a higher grade-level class or by doing advanced curricular materials while in the same class, which is a form of content acceleration.

Eileen: A Sample Compactor Form

Eileen is a fifth grader in a self-contained classroom (Reis, Burns & Renzulli, 1992). Her school, which is very small, is located in a lower socioeconomic urban school district. While Eileen's reading and language scores range between 2 and 5 years above grade level, most of her 29 classmates are reading 1 to 2 years below grade level. This presented Eileen's teacher with a common problem: What is the best way to instruct Eileen?

The teacher agreed to compact her curriculum. Taking the easiest approach possible, the teacher administered all of the unit and level tests in the Holt Basal Language Arts program and excused Eileen from completing the activities and worksheets in the units where she showed proficiency at 80% and above. If Eileen missed one or two questions, the teacher would quickly check for trends in those items; if an error pattern emerged, instruction would be provided to ensure concept mastery. Eileen usually took part in language arts lessons 1 or 2 days a week. The balance of the time she spent with alternative projects, some of which she selected. This strategy spared Eileen up to 8 hours a week of instruction and work in language arts skills that were simply beneath her level. She joined the class instruction only when her pretests indicated she had not fully acquired the skills.

In the time saved through compacting, Eileen engaged in a number of enrichment activities. First, she enjoyed as many as 5 hours a week in a resource room for high ability students. This time was usually scheduled during her language arts class, benefiting both Eileen and her teacher; he didn't have to search for enrichment options because Eileen went to the resource room, and she didn't have make-up assignments because she was not missing essential work. Eileen also visited a regional science center. Science was a second strength area for Eileen, and based on the results of her Interest-A-Lyzer (Renzulli, 1997), famous women were a special interest. Working closely with her teacher, Eileen chose seven biographies of noted women in the science field. All of the books were extremely challenging and locally available. Three were even adult level, but Eileen had no trouble reading them.

Eileen's Compactor, which covered an entire semester, was updated in January. Her teacher remarked that compacting her curriculum had actually saved him time, particularly time he would have spent correcting papers needlessly assigned. The value of compacting for Eileen also convinced him that he should continue the process.

Providing Support for Teachers
to Implement Compacting

In our experiences with curriculum compacting professional development, we have learned that most teachers can implement compacting, but this process is easier for some teachers than for others. Some teachers see the form and read the brief explanation above and are ready to start, while others require more coaching and help. For that reason, we provided an eight-step process in a book we wrote with our colleague, Deborah Burns, about compacting (Reis, Burns, & Renzulli, 1992).

Step 1: Select relevant learning objectives in a subject area or grade level. To select curricular content and learning objectives, teachers may refer to the formal curriculum guides issued by school districts and states or the informal guides provided by textbook publishers.

After locating the objectives, teachers must focus on those that are appropriate for their students. Oftentimes, there's a discrepancy between the objectives noted in the curriculum guides and those actually tested by the school districts. Other objectives may be redundant or overly ambitious. Therefore, teachers should ask the following:

1. To what extent do these objectives represent new learning?

2. Which objectives will best help students increase their use of this content area?

3. Which objectives can be applied to the workplace?

4. Which objectives deal with developing skills or concepts, as opposed to merely memorizing facts?

5. Which objectives are important for high-ability students to understand?

6. Which objectives cannot be learned without formal or sustained instruction?

7. Which objectives reflect the priorities of the school district or state department of education?

After the objectives are selected, they should be listed by priority. Because of their importance, the higher ranked items are the ones on which teachers will concentrate with the entire class, while the less relevant ones are prime candidates for compacting. Simply having a set of learning objectives doesn't tell a teacher how or if these objectives can be adapted to meet students' individual needs. Teachers must know the subject matter, as well as their students' learning styles. The second step in the compacting process can help teachers make these evaluations.

Step 2: Find an appropriate way to pretest the learning objectives. Pretesting, as its name implies, is intended to measure students' skills and talents before instruction begins. It should provide teachers with precise information to answer the following questions:

1. Which objectives have students already met?

2. Which objectives have students not yet attained?

3. Are there any problems that may prevent student progress with the objectives?

Ideally, a pretest should demonstrate whether a student has full, partial, or little mastery of an objective. Objective-referenced tests can do that effectively, as they usually assess one objective at a time through short-answer or multiple-choice responses. On a practical level, these paper-and-pencil tests appeal to teachers because they can be administered in large group settings, require little time to oversee or correct, and are readily available from textbook publishers or testing companies, thus allowing teachers to keep records of students' progress.

Performance-based assessment is a popular alternative to objective-referenced tests. By asking students to do oral, written, or manipulative work in front of them, teachers can observe and evaluate the process students use to arrive at an answer. This procedure is especially successful with younger children who are not yet ready for paper-and-pencil tests. Students may be evaluated individually or in small groups through conferences, interviews, or portfolios of completed work. As with objective-referenced tests, this requires preplanning. Teachers must take the time to locate or create the performance tests, making sure that they're aligned with the desired learning objectives.

Step 3: Identify students who should take the pretests. In the third step, teachers identify students who should participate in the pretesting activity. To do this, they must first discern students' specific strengths, which is critical for two reasons.

First, it ensures that, when students are excused from class for enrichment activities, they're absent only during their curricular strength times. Second, it eliminates the need to assign make-up work when the students return to the classroom. Academic records, standardized tests, class performance, and evaluations from former teachers are all effective means of pinpointing candidates for pretesting. Another method is observation. Teachers should watch for students who complete tasks quickly and accurately, finish reading assignments ahead of their peers, or seem bored or lost in daydreams. Some students will even tell their teachers that the work assigned is too easy, especially if the teachers ask about the different levels of the assignment.

Achievement and aptitude tests can be a valuable gauge of academic ability. By comparing students' subtest scores with local, state, or national norms, educators can see which youngsters fall into the above-average ranges. Since these students usually know more or learn faster than their peers, it's safe to assume that they may benefit from pretesting. National test results confirm the fact that bright students do not necessarily excel in all subject areas. For example, those who score well in math will not always show equal ability in vocabulary. Likewise, students with good vocabulary skills are not always those who do best in reading comprehension.

This underscores the importance of using more than one test and relying on a battery of data to evaluate students' strengths and weaknesses in specific content areas. Teachers must get a total academic picture, and they must also remember that this information leads only to likely candidates for compacting. In other words, just because students perform well in a given area doesn't mean they've mastered all the learning objectives in that area.

What's more, all test instruments are flawed to some degree. Establishing cut-off scores, then, is not an exact science. When it comes to measuring achievement, the debate still rages over "How high is high?" Overall, students who place above the 85th percentile on subtests of norm-referenced achievement tests may be considered viable candidates for compacting. Some teachers may decide that they want to pretest all students in the classroom. These pretests results can be used to organize ad hoc small groups of students with common instructional needs.

Step 4: Pretest students to determine mastery levels. Pretests, both formal and informal, help teachers determine student mastery of course material. But, what constitutes mastery? Since definitions of mastery vary, teachers within the same school should strive to reach a consensus. Deciding how and when to pretest students can be a time-intensive exercise.

One shortcut is to increase the number of students or objectives examined at one time. For example, if a chapter in a math text covers 10 objectives, a small group of students (or the entire class) could be tested on all 10 objectives in one sitting. If small-group testing is not feasible, teachers can follow the same procedures with individual students. Some educators may want to install a permanent "testing table" for this purpose; others may let students score and record their own test results to save time.

Some teachers may want to use performance-based testing. If they choose this form of pretesting, they should observe students closely by taking notes, tracing thought patterns, and posing open-ended questions to assess proficiency with the objectives. Let's assume, for example, that the assignment is to write a persuasive essay. The instructions could be to create and submit an essay that the teacher would read and analyze for content. The teacher could also ask students how they went about organizing their thoughts to see if they truly understand the assignment. Similar sessions can be held to assess other abilities, such as decoding rules, solving problems, or processing science skills. Through these evaluations, many teachers will discover the value of performance-based testing as a supplement to pretesting.

Pretests may also be administered to the entire class. Although it may entail more work for the teacher, it provides the opportunity for all students to demonstrate their strengths in an area. In fact, involving everyone in the process can boost individual confidence and build a stronger sense of community in the classroom. Equipped with a matrix of learning objectives, teachers can fill in the test results and form small, flexible groups based on skill needs.

Mastery levels are bound to fluctuate among students. Youngsters with learning disabilities or visual or hearing impairments, as well as those who are culturally diverse or speak English as a second language must often be evaluated differently than their peers. Consider, for example, a student who demonstrates superior understanding of science concepts. If the goal of compacting is to develop the potential talents of all students, then shouldn't she also be allowed to take part in alternative learning activities even if her spelling and language arts skills are low? There are, in fact, several ways to accomplish this:

1. Try to compact the students in their best content area, even though performance may be below grade level in another content area. Students can spend classroom time, as well as some recess, lunch, or after school time, in alternative activities.

2. Place the students in enrichment programs during the language arts period, since language arts are incorporated into most other subjects. Although students may not be working with the same set of skills as those being taught, they would apply other language arts skills during research, problem-solving, and project-sharing exercises.

Although implementing curriculum compacting for special needs students may be difficult for many teachers, studies have shown that the rewards for both teacher and student justify the hours spent. Engaging these students in the process can elevate self-esteem, foster positive attitudes toward learning, and, in the long-term, improve performance. There are a number of resources that teachers can use to help conduct pretests:

- Reading, math, and other curriculum specialists can assist in identifying learning objectives and student strengths.

- District consultants and teachers of gifted children may be available to help with pretests and other aspects of compacting. This service is especially vital during the first few years, when teachers are trying to organize and implement the compacting program.

- Parent volunteers, aides, and tutors can lend a hand administering tests.

Many companies are also developing new computer technology to pretest and provide individual instruction to targeted students.

Step 5: Streamline practice or instructional time for students who show mastery of the objectives. Students who have a thorough grasp of the learning objectives should be allowed to take part in enrichment or acceleration activities during class time. This exposes them to material that is not only new and stimulating, but more closely aligned to their learning rates and abilities.

For illustration purposes, let's say that a student has mastered three out of five objectives in a given unit. It follows, then, that the student should not take part in the classroom instruction of those three objectives. Depending upon the teacher, some students may be excused from specific class sessions (e.g., the Monday and Wednesday portions of vocabulary building), while others may forego certain chapters or pages in the text or specific sets of learning activities.

Step 6: Provide small-group or individualized instruction for students who have not yet mastered all the objectives, but are capable of doing so more quickly than their classmates. Teachers can provide differentiated opportunities to instruct high–potential students who qualify for compacting, but have not yet mastered all the objectives. This may enable teachers to have fewer groups in their classrooms.

Content compacting differs from skills compacting. As the name implies, it compresses overall course material that students have already mastered or are able to master in a fraction of the normal time. Skills compacting, on the other hand, eliminates specific skills that students have already acquired. Content compacting is also designed for general knowledge subjects (e.g., social studies, science, and literature), whereas skills compacting is intended for mathematics, spelling, grammar, and language mechanics.

Of the two, skills compacting is easier to accomplish. Pretesting is a simpler process, and mastery can be documented more efficiently. Content compacting, on the other hand, is more flexible, as students can absorb the material at their own speed. In content compacting, the means of evaluation are also less formal; teachers may require an essay, an interview, or an open-ended short answer test (Karnes & Bean, 2004).

Step 7: Offer academic alternatives for students whose curriculum has been compacted. Alternatives often exist to provide acceleration, enrichment, or both for students whose curriculum has been compacted. This step is often the most challenging and the most creative for teachers. The possibilities for replacement activities include:

- providing an accelerated curriculum based on advanced concepts;

- offering more challenging content (alternative texts, fiction or nonfiction works);

- adapting classwork to individual curricular needs or learning styles;

- initiating individual or small-group projects using contracts or management plans;

- using interest or learning centers;

- providing opportunities for self-directed learning or decision making;

- offering minicourses on research topics or other high-interest areas;

- establishing small seminar groups for advanced studies;

- using mentors to guide in learning advanced content or pursuing independent studies; and

- providing units or assignments that are self-directed, such as creative writing, game creation, and creative and critical thinking training.

Teachers will have to decide which replacement activities to use, and their decisions will be based on factors such as time, space, resources, school policy, and help from other faculty (such as a gifted program teacher or a library media specialist). But, while practical concerns should be considered, what should ultimately determine replacement activities are the degree of academic challenge *and* the students' interests. When students understand that, if they demonstrate proficiency, they will earn time to pursue their own interests, they will often work to earn this opportunity. Our role as teachers is to escalate the challenge level of the material students are pursuing in order to provide adequate academic challenges. Additional suggested alternatives for students are provided after Step 8.

Step 8: Keep records of the compacting process and instructional options for compacted students. Any differentiated program requires added record keeping. Unlike a regular classroom where all students are on the same page or exercise at any given time, teachers who provide a compacted curriculum have students doing different assignments at different levels and at different times. Keeping concise records, then, is essential, and it can be time-consuming without proper planning. Teachers and administrators should collectively decide how the compacting process should be documented, and all written documentation should include these basics:

1. student strength areas, as verified by test scores or performance;

2. the pretests used to determine mastery and the learning objectives that were eliminated; and

3. recommended enrichment and acceleration activities.

The Compactor form was designed expressly to track the compacting process. Teachers employed in states with mandates for gifted education may be able to substitute the Compactor form for the Individual Education Plan (IEP), thus curbing the paperwork required for state-funded services. No matter what record-keeping vehicle they use, it's critical that teachers thoroughly chronicle the compacting process. The facts and figures they compile can be used in parent-teacher files. They can also be included in students' permanent academic records. The information can even help win support for compacting when the idea is being "sold," since people tend to react more favorably to issues presented in a written format.

The most challenging part of compacting is deciding what students should do with time they have earned. In deciding which curricular alternatives to use, teachers should first list all the enrichment and acceleration activities available in their school districts. These can be organized around five major areas:

1. *classroom activities*—independent or small-group study; escalated coverage of the regular curriculum; mini-courses; special interest groups; clubs; interest development centers; and special lessons for furthering cognitive and affective processes;

2. *resource room and special class programs*—these include the same activities as above, but are often held in locations outside of the classroom and may be taught by special teachers;

3. *accelerated studies*—grade-skipping; honors and Advanced

Placement courses; college classes; summer or evening classes; early admission to kindergarten or first grade; cross-grade grouping; continuous progress curricula; and special seminars;

4. *out-of-school experiences*—internships; mentorships; work study programs; and community programs, such as theater and symphonic groups, artists' workshops, and museum programs;

5. *district, school, or departmental programs*—encompasses the options above, plus correspondence courses and programs for independent study, special counseling, career education, and library studies.

Enrichment Materials in the Classroom

Gifted education teachers or enrichment specialists are excellent sources for enrichment activities. The services they supply range from alternative teaching units or materials, to mentoring student projects. For teachers who don't have access to these specialists, there are a host of commercially published materials on the market. These kits, books, and activity cards, which offer high quality at reasonable prices, can be adapted to individuals or small student groups of all ages.

Student interests are key in choosing enrichment or acceleration options. When asked what they enjoy most about compacting, children consistently cite the freedom to select their own topics of study. Although we commonly assume that, when a student excels in a given area, he or she has a special interest in it, but this is not always true. Often, students perform well in a course because they've been directed and rewarded by parents and teachers. Students may also lean toward one academic area simply because they've had little exposure to others. Still, if a youngster is outstanding in math, for example, the teacher should try to promote further interest in the subject. A good way to do this is to suggest an accelerated math activity; if the student and parents agree to it, they should proceed. If, however, the student would rather work on a self-initiated project, then the teacher should try to accommodate those wishes while also considering how to provide an appropriate level of challenge.

The Interest-A-Lyzer (Renzulli, 1997) is a 13-item questionnaire designed to help students examine and focus their interests. Basically, students are asked to imagine themselves in a series of real and hypothetical situations and then relate how they would react. The primary purpose of this exercise is to stimulate thought and discussion. Students not only come to know themselves better, but also get a chance to share their discoveries with both teachers and peers.

Teachers play a dual role in fostering student interests. Once they've identified general categories of interest, they must refine and focus them, then provide students with creative and productive outlets for expressing them. A child who enjoys rock music, for instance, may want to become a musician. But, there are other avenues students can pursue, as well, such as that of radio announcer or concert producer. Teachers must be sensitive to students' talents and inclinations within their fields of interests while, at the same time, encouraging them to explore a range of options within those fields.

Creating interest development centers is also an effective strategy. Unlike traditional learning centers that focus on basic skills, interest centers invite students to investigate topics within a general theme, such as bicycling or the education of people with hearing impairments. Shelves, therefore, must be stocked with manipulative, activity-oriented tools. Videos, pamphlets, magazine articles, books, slides, and display items are all standard fare. Resources that introduce children to research skills, not just reference skills, are valuable, too. An interest center on bicycling, for example, could feature texts on how to make a bike path, seek city council permission to erect public bike racks, or plan a bike safety rodeo.

Once teachers have set up the center, they should formally "unveil" it to their students. A 20-minute session revolving around a film, speaker, or discussion is generally all it takes to enthuse children about the new resource. Not all students will want to explore every interest center topic. But, when several centers are established over the school year, most youngsters delve into at least one activity. Evaluating students' interest inventories should help teachers launch projects that appeal to the majority of students.

Perhaps the most critical success factor, however, is the teacher's attitude. If teachers insist that only students who finish their work can use the center, then some students will erroneously equate center activities with skill development. On the other hand, those teachers who allocate time for all students to enjoy center projects send the message that exploratory and creative pursuits are just as valuable as textbook and worksheet assignments. Encouraging children to be risk takers and information gatherers reinforces important behaviors that lead to a love of independent learning.

Research on Curriculum Compacting

A national study completed at the University of Connecticut's National Research Center on the Gifted and Talented (NRC/GT; Reis et al., 1992) examined the use of curriculum compacting for use with students from a wide diversity of school districts. Participants in the study included 465 second- through sixth-grade classroom teachers from 27 school districts throughout the country. Classroom teachers were randomly assigned to participate in either the treatment (implemented compacting) or the control group (continued with normal teaching practices). Treatment and control group teachers were asked to target one or two candidates in their classrooms for curriculum compacting, and all participating students in treatment and control groups were tested before and after treatment with above-level Iowa Tests of Basic Skills (ITBS). Next-grade-level tests were used to compensate for the "topping out" ceiling effect that is frequently encountered when measuring the achievement of high-ability students.

The most important finding from this study might be described as the more-for-less phenomenon. Approximately 40–50% of traditional classroom material was compacted for targeted students in one or more content areas. When teachers eliminated as much as 50% of regular curricular activities and materials for targeted students, no differences were observed in posttest achievement scores between treatment and control groups in math concepts, math computation, social studies, and spelling. In science, the students who had 40–50% of their curriculum eliminated actually scored significantly higher on science achievement posttests than their peers in the control group. Likewise, students whose curriculum was specifically compacted in mathematics scored significantly higher than their peers in the control group on the math concepts posttest. These findings point out the benefits of compacting for increases on standard achievement assessments. Analyses of data related to replacement activities also indicated that students viewed these activities as much more challenging than standard material.

The vast majority of teachers were able to implement curriculum compacting for the student(s) they selected, although many experienced some frustration. They were challenged by a lack of expertise in knowing what to substitute for high-ability students, limited time for planning how to meet individual differences, and the logistics of teaching different topics to different groups of students. Some also indicated the lack of support staff needed to implement replacement activities (reading and math specialists, gifted and talented program staff) and other concerns relating to classroom management.

While curriculum compacting is a viable process for meeting the needs of high-ability students in the regular classroom, it does takes time, effort, and planning on the part of classroom teachers. With urban teachers, especially those who work with students placed at risk because of poverty, compacting requires different types of efforts, particularly in finding different materials to substitute in environments that often rely primarily on addressing deficits and remedial instruction. Many factors contribute to the creation of a supportive school environment for the use of curriculum compacting: administrative support and encouragement, availability of materials and resources for substitution of the regular curriculum, the availability of guided practice and coaching, and teachers' increased ease and reflections about how to fit compacting into their professional practices.

In a follow-up study (Reis et al., 1993), a substantial number of teachers involved in the study indicated that they were able to extend curriculum compacting to other students, many of whom were not identified and involved in the gifted program. This finding may indicate the usefulness of extending the types of gifted education pedagogy often reserved for high-ability students to a larger segment of the population, as has been previously suggested (Renzulli & Reis, 1991), and the need to extend differentiation services to a broader segment of the school population (Renzulli & Reis, 1997).

In the follow-up study (Reis et al., 1993), teachers were asked to use both curriculum compacting and self-selected Type III enrichment projects (Renzulli, 1977a) based on students' interests as a systematic intervention for a diverse group of underachieving talented students. In this study, underachievement was reversed in the majority of students. The use of compacting and high-interest projects (Renzulli) specifically targets student strengths and interests to cause this reversal (Baum, Renzulli, & Hébert, 1995).

Advice From Successful Teachers
Who Implement Compacting

Research (Reis, et al., 1993) has indicated that the most successful teachers to use compacting implemented the following strategies.

First, they worked with a colleague or colleagues with whom they shared a common bond. They wanted to improve their teaching practices and were not afraid to ask each other for help or support.

Second, they started with a small group of students and not their entire class. The successful teachers understood that this process would take some time and organization and became committed to working with a group of students who really needed the process first. By not trying this with all students, they reduced the stress and challenges they would have encountered if they tried to do too much in the beginning of the process.

Third, they asked for help from their liaisons, the district content consultants, and each other. In each successful district, teachers asked each other how they were handling pretesting and assessment. They shared strategies for management and replacement and visited each other's classrooms at their own suggestions or because a liaison suggested it. The modeling and sharing of success stories made a difference.

Fourth, they also understood that, like a novice practicing piano scales, they would continue to improve by trying and reflecting on their work in this area. The teachers who did the best work consistently asked their colleagues and liaisons what had worked best and how current practices could extend and improve this practice. By reflecting on what had worked, they were able to modify and change their own attempts and consistently improve. In the most successful schools, teachers were provided with time to work with liaisons, small amounts of material funds for curricular replacement costs, and substitutes to enable them to visit and observe direct modeling in each other's classrooms.

Summary

The many changes faced in today's schools require all educators to examine a broad range of techniques for providing equitably for *all* students. Curriculum compacting is one such process. It is not tied to a specific content area or grade level, nor is it aligned with a particular approach to school or curricular reform. Rather, the process is adaptable to any school organizational plan or curricular framework, and it is flexible enough to be used within the context of rapidly changing approaches to general education. The research described in this publication and the practical experiences gained through several years of field testing and refining the compacting process, particularly in urban areas and in schools that serve culturally diverse students, have demonstrated the many positive benefits of using this process for both teachers and students, particularly talented students who may be placed at risk for underachieving in school.

Like any innovation, curriculum compacting requires time, energy, and acceptance from teachers. Yet, educators we have studied who compact effectively have indicated that it takes no longer than normal teaching practices. More importantly, they reported that the benefits to all students certainly make the effort worthwhile. One teacher's comment about the process reflects the attitude of most teachers who have participated in research about compacting: "As soon as I saw how enthusiastic and receptive my students were about the compacting process, I began to become more committed to implementing this method in all my classes."

Frequently Asked Questions and Answers
About Curriculum Compacting

Q. What is required before you start compacting?

A. To compact effectively, you must have (1) a clear understanding of your curricular objectives and (2) knowledge of
which students have already mastered those objectives or
are capable of mastering them in less time. It also helps to
have some background information on compacting itself
and an idea of the pretest devices and alternative activities
you plan to use. *Curriculum Compacting: The Complete Guide
to Modifying the Regular Curriculum for High Ability Students*
(Reis, Burns, & Renzulli, 1992) provides in-depth coverage of the subject. This book is available from Creative
Learning Press, P.O. Box 320, Mansfield Center, CT
06250. In addition, a 1-hour videotape of satellite training
by Sally Reis is available from The National Research
Center on the Gifted and Talented at the University of
Connecticut.

Q. What type of staff development is initially necessary?

A. Teachers and staff should first get a general overview of compacting. Creative Learning Press has videotapes specially produced for this purpose; there is also an outstanding book on the subject entitled *It's About Time: Inservice Strategies for Curriculum Compacting* (1986) by Alane Starko. After everyone's been oriented to compacting, they should meet to determine learning objectives, methods of pretesting, and other critical elements in the process. Additionally, teachers should try to observe, within a classroom setting, other teachers who successfully compact the curriculum.

Q. Can classroom teachers compact the curriculum without the help of teachers who work with gifted children?

A. Yes! In fact, classroom teachers bear the primary responsibility for implementing the compacting process. But, if teachers of the gifted are available, they can ease the job by procuring enrichment resources or upgrading the challenge level of the regular curricular materials.

Q. What about administrative support? Should I tell my administrator about my decision to compact?

A. Absolutely. We feel that most administrators will be supportive; but, because compacting is such a major innovation, it's essential that they be consulted before you begin. Doing this may prompt your administrator to ask other teachers to participate.

Q. Should parents be informed if their child's curriculum has been compacted?

A. We want parents to be active partners in compacting and,

therefore, strongly recommend that they be notified once it's been initiated. A good way to do this is through a brief letter that describes the process. Parents should understand, for example, that compacting may change the amount or type of paperwork their children bring home.

Q. What should I tell my class about compacting?

A. Compacting should be explained in simple terms to all students. Among the points you should touch upon are pretests, the fact that some students may already know the material being tested, and that exciting learning activities exist for students who have already mastered the material. You should also communicate in advance the rules regarding behavior while students are doing alternative work. Two such rules may include working as quietly as possible and not interrupting the teacher while he or she instructs the rest of the class.

Q. At what grade level should compacting be introduced?

A. The ideal time to start compacting is as soon as children enter school. It has been found that, when the process begins in kindergarten, youngsters learn to use their independent time more appropriately and they choose more suitable enrichment activities. Similarly, it's often easier to compact in an elementary classroom than it is in a secondary class. Elementary teachers generally see students perform for a larger block of time and in more than one subject area. Secondary teachers, on the other hand, may only see students for one 50-minute session a day. This gives them more of a challenge.

Q. What are the least difficult subject areas to compact?

A. Usually, skill areas with highly sequential curricular organization, such as spelling, mathematics, and grammar, are the least difficult to compact. Once you're familiar with the process, you may compact any subject area. Teachers have even reported wonderful results in art and music.

Q. Am I correct in assuming that, if I teach process writing or use a whole-language approach, compacting is unnecessary?

A. No. With process writing, youngsters who master the writing objectives for their grade level shouldn't just move up another difficulty notch, as is often the case. Instead, they should be allowed to pursue enrichment assignments or projects of their choice. The same holds true for the whole-language approach. If students show mastery of the learning objectives, simply replacing time with grade-level trade books, for example, may not be the best option. The alternatives presented must be challenging and keyed to students' interests.

Q. Is it better to compact by time period (every marking period, for instance) or by instructional unit?

A. Compacting by instructional unit is best. A "unit" generally refers to an instructional period that revolves around a theme, chronological time period, or a set of academic objectives. For example, to compact a sixth-grade unit on *Johnny Tremaine*, the teacher would modify the curriculum for students who have either read the novel or who could read and master the learning objectives more quickly than their classmates. At the elementary level, teachers frequently compact a basic skills unit of instruction, such as the teaching of long division.

Q. Do you recommend compacting an entire semester, leaving the last 2 months free for student self-selected projects, or compacting 2½ days a week, leaving the rest of the time for alternative work?

A. Most teachers prefer to compact 2 or 3 days a week and set aside 1 or 2 days or short blocks of time for enrichment assignments. When you compact a semester, it demands tremendous time and energy to plan a full 2 months of enrichment options.

Q. Will I be more successful if I initially compact one student's curriculum instead of a whole group's?

A. Teachers have effectively compacted the curriculum for individual students, but the students often feel uncomfortable being singled out. It's better, then, to start with a small group. Working with several students doesn't demand much more time or many more resources than working with one student.

Q. If I compact for my high-ability students and let them leave the class for alternative activities, won't the quality of my classroom discussions suffer?

A. Many teachers have expressed this concern, which is merited to some degree. However, we must also remember that less-able students are sometimes intimidated by the presence of brighter students and, consequently, won't contribute to the discussions. To resolve the problem, teachers might try some classroom sessions with the gifted students and some without them; if the discussions succeed better with the advanced students, then it makes sense to include them.

Q. Do students who are not in the gifted program ever benefit from compacting?

A. Yes, most definitely. According to our field tests, many average students get great value from curriculum compacting in one or more content areas. We believe that the compacting process actually helps reverse the "dumbing down" of the curriculum, which benefits all students, as do the enrichment materials brought into the classroom for use during compacted time.

Q. Can lower ability students take part in enrichment opportunities?

A. All students, regardless of ability, should be given time to enjoy enrichment opportunities. Everyone would agree that every student should, in fact, learn problem solving, creative thinking skills, and other facets of process training that alternative activities provide (Karnes & Bean, 2004). Teachers could schedule a special time for these activities, such as Friday afternoons.

Q. Should the curriculum be compacted for underachievers?

A. Underachievers should be considered for compacting. Youngsters who underachieve are often bright students who are bored with the regular curriculum. In many instances, they've also discovered that finishing their lessons before their classmates only means that they're assigned more of the same work. Case studies have shown that compacting can break this unproductive cycle. By directing underachievers to more challenging work, rather than simply extra work, we give them an incentive to excel.

Q. How do I grade when I compact the curriculum?

A. You should grade on the regular curriculum, which has been compacted. In our opinion, grades should reflect mastery of content and not time spent in a subject area. However, when you substitute independent study, we don't think it should be graded. Our preference is to provide some qualitative, holistic evaluation of the work completed. Note: If you find that students are not using their time for alternative study wisely, you should discuss the problem with them. You might reiterate the concept of compacting and explain what the next step would be if behavior doesn't change (such as a parent meeting). Compacting represents a radical educational departure for most students, and it takes time for them to adjust.

Q. Is there a way to reorganize the physical classroom space to make compacting easier?

A. Yes! You can set up "student stations" and interest centers consisting of a desk or table with two or three chairs for independent study or free reading. A small, comfortable library corner, or special learning or interest centers, can also be established.

Q. How expensive is compacting to implement?

A. To facilitate compacting, you'll need additional resources. You may have to order pretests and other instruments to measure proficiency. And, if your students don't have access to a gifted specialist, you'll have to arrange in-class activities for them instead. With as little as $800 in start-up funds and an annual budget of $200 per building, you can start and maintain a library of enrichment resources. These items can be loaned to classrooms as needed.

Language Arts Web Sites

Just For Kids: Gifted Child Recommended Reading List
http://www.just-for-kids.com/gifted.html

This Web site focuses on the unique learning needs of precocious readers. Specifically, the author provides extensive lists of
books that are psychologically and developmentally appropriate
for young (age 7–10), but advanced readers. The author organ-
izes her recommendations into eight categories: Picture Books,
Chapter Books, Timeless Fantasy, Classic Stories, Modern
Fiction 1, Modern Fiction 2, Epic Fantasy, and Nonfiction.

EDSITEment
http://edsitement.neh.gov

EDSITEment contains many sites in the areas of literature, history, foreign languages, and art history. The sites are selected

using a review process developed by the National Endowment for the Humanities, so they are truly among the top sites for humanities learning and research. Under the broad category of Literature, more than 25 different links are available on diverse literary topics, including American Verse Project (electronic archive of American poetry prior to 1920); Mark Twain and His Times (broad range of materials on the author and the era in which he lived); Presidential Speeches (documentary resources dedicated to American Presidents); and Victorian Women Writers Project (texts and contexts for students of 19th-century British literature).

American Library Association's Book Links

http://www.ala.org/Content/NavigationMenu/Products_and_ Publications/Periodicals/Book_Links/Book_Links.htm

This Web site provides all students, including those who are advanced readers and writers, with the opportunity to explore a self-selected topic in depth. Precocious readers may want to pursue an author study about their favorite writer or illustrator. *Book Links*, a magazine designed for teachers, librarians, and media specialists, publishes author studies, essays linking books on a similar theme, bibliographies, retrospective reviews, and other features for those who educate young people. Several Web sites feature renowned authors and illustrators and invite browsers to explore books, as well as their authors. Some provide students with the opportunity to communicate directly with selected authors.

National Counsel of Teachers of English (NCTE)

http://www.ncte.org

The homepage for the NCTE provides resources for elementary, middle, and secondary teachers, including a clearinghouse of links to sites that provide information and ideas for curricula, as well as information on the organization itself.

International Reading Association (IRA)
http://www.reading.org

This site contains a variety of documents. The first is the IRA's set of Children's Reading Rights, and the second contains the national standards for English Language Arts. A third site contains three lists of "best books": Teachers' Choices, 1999 (an annotated list of more than 25 books); Young Adults' Choices, 1999 (more than 30 books with annotations); and Children's Choices, 1999 (more than 70 books with annotations, categorized for beginning, young, intermediate, and advanced readers).

The Center for the Improvement of Early Reading Achievement (CIERA)
http://www.ciera.org/index.html

This site contains free information about early literacy acquisition and effective strategies for teaching reading. CIERA publications provide insight into the current thinking of the nation's leading researchers in the field of literacy. The site also contains links to a broad range of literacy-related sites.

Bibliotherapy
http://www.ci.eugene.or.us/Library/staffref/therapy.htm

Bibliotherapy is the use of children's books to help young people understand and resolve personal issues. It is a particularly effective technique with avid readers because they are capable of seeing the implications of the material not only for the characters in the plot, but also for themselves. This Web site provides a list of books for helping children of all ages deal with a variety of issues.

Author Studies for Primary Grades (1–3) Language Arts
http://edservices.aea7.k12.ia.us/edtech/teacherpages/djjwolf

This site enables primary students to explore the relationship between reading and writing through exploring the stories and characters of renowned children's authors and illustrators. The site offers biographies and contact information for many of the authors, as well as hands-on activities designed to appeal to both the visually and verbally gifted.

Math and Science Web Sites

Eisenhower National Clearinghouse (ENC)
http://enc.org

ENC is a top-shelf repository for current mathematics and science resources. The site is a consistent award winner because it is well maintained and packed to the roof with math and science information. Sites include lessons, activities, interactive Web sites, and journal articles. Some of the site links include Digital Dozen (13 of the best-of-the-best science and mathematics sites, selected each month), Innovator of the Month (a spotlight on educators who are reinventing learning with their students), ENC Focus (select resources for teaching current, hot topics), and Lessons & Activities (Web sites to either supplement existing curricula or integrate into the classroom).

Internet Detectives
http://www.madison.k12.wi.us/tnl/detectives

This project was formerly a biweekly publication produced through a cooperative effort of 12 classrooms around the U.S. It has since been formalized within the Madison Metropolitan School District and now goes by the name of Internet Detectives. Since 1996–1997, students have amassed an archive of sites in science, mathematics, and history, including, for example, Inventions, the Holocaust, and Natural Disasters. Selection criteria are included for readers and can be used by other students who want to use similar criteria for identifying and selecting Internet sites for their own Web pages.

NASA For Kids

http://www.wff.nasa.gov/~code850/pages/kidslinks.html

The National Aeronautics and Space Administration (NASA) maintains an award-winning Web site with a variety of links and pages designed for young people. Students can access a variety of rich Web sites on topics such as the Mars Millennium Project, space travel, the National Air and Space Museum, and science news.

Math Forum

http://mathforum.org

This site offers a comprehensive list of resources for students and teachers, including math resources by subject, advanced and college-level math materials, and a rich student section, including weekly challenges and math tips and tricks. This site is a must for differentiation at all levels of mathematics—and for students with a mathematical bent.

TERC

http://www.terc.edu

TERC is a not-for-profit education and research and development organization dedicated to improving mathematics and science learning. Their Web site contains links to TERC projects in which students can get involved, as well as TERC papers, which explore a variety of innovative instructional strategies related to math and science teaching. A most notable link takes browsers to *Hands-On,* a publication devoted to applying hands-on, inquiry-based learning to classrooms. The practical, down-to-earth articles written by practitioners are inspirational and easy to adapt.

The Exploratorium
http://www.exploratorium.edu

The Exploratorium's Web site, which is available in four languages, is as interactive and hands-on as the museum in San Francisco. Thus, it's not surprising that the Web site has earned a variety of awards. Monthly, the staff presents "10 Cool Sites" in science, art, and education. Sample sites include Neuroscience for Kids, Calendars Through the Ages, Citizen Kurchatov, DNA for Dinner, Project Primary, Understanding Color, Project Full Moon, and The Learning Matters of Chemistry.

The Mathman
http://www.shout.net/~mathman

This Web site uses real-world problems to illustrate mathematical topics such as graphs and equations. One link includes sample calculus lessons for elementary students. Much of the information is predicated upon a text and worksheets that can be ordered through the site.

Chance
http://www.dartmouth.edu/~chance

This database contains material designed to help teach a Chance course. It was developed cooperatively by Middlebury College, Grinnell College, Spelman College, the University of California–San Diego, the University of Minnesota, and Dartmouth. The aim of the database is to make students more informed, crucial readers of current news that uses probability and statistics. A discussion site is included.

Fibonacci Numbers and the Golden Section
http://www.mcs.surrey.ac.uk/Personal/R.Knott/Fibonacci/fib.html

This is an award-winning site that contains more than 200 pages of information about Fibonacci numbers, the golden section, and golden string. Categories of information include Fibonacci numbers and Golden sections in nature, the puzzling world of Fibonacci numbers, the intriguing mathematical world of Fibonacci and Phi, the Golden string, applications of Fibonacci numbers and Phi, and resources and links.

Ask a Biologist
http://askabiologist.asu.edu/research/index.html

This Web site, which is geared toward high school biology students and teachers, allows teachers and students to ask biologists questions pertaining to anything in the biological sciences. You type in your name, school, grade, e-mail address, and question and submit it. You will then get a response to your question from a biologist. Also included are various articles and a gallery in which you have to guess what the images are. There are also links to other Web sites that can help students with homework, science fair projects, resources like dictionaries, or general knowledge in biology, as well as links for lesson plans. The interactive site is easy to navigate and appealing to the eye, and it is a SafeSurf site, which protects students from the privacy and ethical issues that go along with using the Internet.

Net Frog
http://curry.edschool.virginia.edu/go/frog

This Web site, which is aimed at high school students and teachers, consists of a tutorial that allows you to dissect a frog without using a real frog. It also has links to other resources that allow you to compare the frog anatomy with human anatomy and also learn about a frog's habitat. This site had many strengths. First, it is easy to navigate; the links are easy to access and the site is visually pleasing. Second, it goes through the entire dissection of a real frog and allows you to use many methods, such as pictures, text, narratives, and videos to learn about the anatomy of the frog. It is a great tool for teachers because it can be used to prepare students for doing a dissection or function as an alternative to doing one.

Mentorships/Telementoring

Provide mentorships for students with a passion in science. Mentors can be located at local universities/community colleges, online, in the business sector, and among parents of young people. Some good online mentorship sites include:

Scientific America
http://www.sciam.com/askexpert_directory.cfm

Electronic Emissary
http://emissary.wm.edu

Telementoring Program
http://www.telementor.org

Social Studies Web Sites

National Council for the Social Studies (NCSS)
http://www.ncss.org

This Web site is an extensive resource for social studies education. The homepage is a gateway to hundreds of pages of teacher resources in history, politics and government, geography, anthropology, economics, political science, and sociology. One link on the homepage is dedicated to the social studies standards, sometimes referred to as the ten social studies themes (e.g., culture, individual identity and development, global connections). Browsers who visit each theme are provided with links to Internet resources that support each standard. Other homepage links to student projects are plentiful and inspiring.

History Matters

http://www.historymatters.gmu.edu

This Web site is a project of the American Social History Center and is designed for high school and college teachers of U.S. history survey courses. It is a gateway to Web resources and offers unique teaching materials, first-person primary documents, and threaded discussions on teaching U.S. history. Many Pasts, one of the links, provides browsers with inspiring descriptions of research-based projects that have been completed by students. For example, "What Did You Do in the War, Grandma?" was conducted by 17 Rhode Island students. They interviewed 36 Rhode Island women who recalled their lives in the years before, during, and after World War II.

Connecticut Historical Society

http://www.chs.org

The Connecticut Historical Society, located in Hartford, maintains an extensive and noteworthy Web site. Their homepage links to a variety of pages, including History Day, museums, historical fact sites, and their library, which houses 100,000 volumes and 3,000,000 manuscripts, including many rare books and handwritten material such as diaries and letters. The library is surpassed only by its graphics collection, which contains more than 200,000 photographs, prints, and drawings of Connecticut people, places, and events. Teachers may contact the staff members in Hartford, who are eager to help teachers and students with any aspect of historical research.

American Memory Historical Collection

http://memory.loc.gov

The American Memory Historical Collection, a major component of the National Digital Library Program, is composed of digitized documents, photographs, recorded sound, moving pictures, and text. There are more than 70 collections, some of which investigate themes such as elections, immigration, inaugurations, Presidents, and women pioneers.

The History Net
http://www.thehistorynet.com

This site allows you to explore the discoveries and inventions that have changed thinking and history. Some examples include mapmaking and its role in exploration; photography and the printing press and their ability to preserve the past; railroads and their ability to bridge people and continents; and telescopes and their ability to see into the past and future.

Teaching About Turning Points in History
http://nationalhistoryday.org/03_educators/2000/teaching.htm

This site provides teachers with strategies and resources to encourage students to think critically about turning points in history and to conduct research about historically significant topics that interest them.

Contests and Competitions Web Sites

Encourage students to participate in contests and competitions relating to their areas of interest, such as those in the list below. Other contests and competitions are listed in *All the Best Contests for Kids* (5th ed.) by Joan Bergstrom and Craig Bergstom, *The Ultimate Guide to Student Contests, Grades 7–12,* by Scott Pendleton, and *Competitions: Maximizing Your Abilities,* by Frances Karnes and Tracy Riley. Contests and competitions are listed and described by grade level and content areas. To size up a competition, use the following guidelines:

1. Match contest objectives with the grade-level district objectives.

2. Ensure that the contest product strengthens connections in science and other subject areas.

3. Match the contest with the age level and interests of the students.

4. Ensure that the contest has a workable deadline for entries in relationship to the school calendar.

5. Determine what materials will be purchased by the school and what materials will need to be provided by parents or local industry. (Beltac, 1999)

History Day
http://www.nationalhistoryday.org

This national contest provides students with an opportunity to develop a project on a historical topic of their choice. Students in grades 6–12 select a topic within the yearly theme (examples include "Exploration, Encounter, Exchange in History" and "Rights and Responsibilities in History") and develop a project in any of several categories, including individual paper, group or individual exhibit, and group or individual documentary.

Continental Mathematics League
http://continentalmathleague.hostrack.com

This site provides information on the CML contests, including math contests for grades 4–9, a high school calculus league, and a Java computer contest, as well as links to a variety of other sites, including the National Science League and the National Social Studies League.

Mathematical Olympiads
for Elementary and Middle Schools
http://www.moems.org

Mathematical Olympiad is a contest for students in grades 4–8 (Division M is grades 4–6, Division E is grades 7–8) designed to encourage students' enjoyment of math by exposing them to nonroutine math challenges. The five timed competitions take place in the students' home schools from November to March.

Problem of the Day, Problem of the Week

Institute a "Problem of the Day" or "Problem of the Week." Gather problems from past competitions of Continental Math League or Math Olympiad, for example. Additional resources for math problem books:

MindWare
http://www.mindwareonline.com/mwstore/index.cfm

Marcy Cook
http://www.marcycookmath.com

References

Archambault, F. X., Jr., Westberg, K. L., Brown, S., Hallmark, B. W., Emmons, C., & Zhang, W. (1993). *Regular classroom practices with gifted students: Results of a national survey of classroom teachers.* Storrs: The National Research Center on the Gifted and Talented, University of Connecticut.

Baum, S. M., Renzulli, J. S., & Hébert, T. P. (1995). Reversing underachievement: Creative productivity as a systematic intervention. *Gifted Child Quarterly, 39*, 224–235.

Beltac, T. F. (1999). Sizing up science competitions. *Science and Children, 37*(1), 24–27.

Karnes, F. A. & Bean, S. M. (2004). *Process skills rating scales–Revised.* Waco, TX: Prufrock Press.

Reis, S. M., Burns, D. E., & Renzulli, J. S. (1992). *Curriculum compacting: The complete guide to modifying the regular curriculum for high ability students.* Mansfield Center, CT: Creative Learning Press.

Reis, S. M., Westberg, K. L., Kulikowich, J., Caillard, F., Hébert, T. P., Purcell, J. H., Rogers, J., Smist, J., & Plucker,

J. A. (1992). *Technical report of the curriculum compacting study.* Storrs: The National Research Center on the Gifted and Talented, University of Connecticut.

Reis, S. M., Westberg, K. L., Kulikowich, J., Caillard, F., Hébert, T., Purcell, J. H., Rogers, J., Smist, J. & Plucker, J. (1993). *An analysis of the impact of curriculum compacting on classroom practices: Technical report.* Storrs: The National Research Center on the Gifted and Talented, University of Connecticut.

Renzulli, J. S. (1977a). *The enrichment triad model: A guide for developing defensible programs for the gifted and talented.* Mansfield Center, CT: Creative Learning Press.

Renzulli, J. S. (1977b). *The interest-a-lyzer.* Mansfield Center, CT: Creative Learning Press.

Renzulli, J. S. (1988). The multiple-menu model for developing differentiated curriculum for the gifted and talented. *Gifted Child Quarterly, 32*, 298–309.

Renzulli, J. S. (1997). *Interest-a-lyzer family of instruments: A manual for teachers.* Mansfield Center, CT: Creative Learning Press.

Renzulli, J. S., & Reis, S. M. (1991). The reform movement and the quiet crisis in gifted education. *Gifted Child Quarterly, 35*, 26–35.

Renzulli, J. S., & Reis, S. M. (1997). *The schoolwide enrichment model: A comprehensive plan for educational excellence.* Mansfield Center, CT: Creative Learning Press.

Renzulli, J. S., & Smith, L. H. (1978). *The compactor.* Mansfield Center, CT: Creative Learning Press.

Southern, T. W., & Jones, E. D. (1992). The real problems with academic acceleration. *Gifted Child Today, 15*(2), 34–38.

Stanley, J. C. (1989). A look back at educational non–acceleration: An international tragedy. *Gifted Child Today, 12*(4), 60–61.

Starko, A. (1986). *It's about time: Inservice strategies for curriculum compacting.* Mansfield Center, CT: Creative Learning Press.

Tomlinson, C. A. (1995). *How to differentiate instruction in mixed-ability classrooms*. Alexandria, VA: Association for Supervision and Curriculum Development.

Tomlinson, C. A. (2000). *Differentiation of instruction in the elementary grades* (Report No. ED 443572). Champaign, IL: ERIC Clearinghouse on Elementary and Early Childhood Education.

Westberg, K. L., Archambault, F. X., Dobyns, S. M., & Salvin, T. J. (1993). *Technical report: An observational study of instructional and curricular practices used with gifted and talented students in regular classrooms*. Storrs: The National Research Center on the Gifted and Talented, University of Connecticut.

About the Authors

Sally M. Reis is a professor and the head of the Educational Psychology Department in the Neag School of Education at the University of Connecticut, where she also serves as principal investigator of the National Research Center on the Gifted and Talented. She has also been a classroom teacher in public education, as well as an administrator. She has authored more than 130 articles, 11 books, 40 book chapters, and numerous monographs and technical reports and worked in a research team that has generated more than $35 million in grants in the last 15 years. Her research interests are related to talent development in all children, as well as special populations of gifted and talented students. She is also interested in extensions of the Schoolwide Enrichment Model for both gifted students and as a way to identify talent and potential in students who have not been previously identified as gifted.

Joseph Renzulli is the Neag Professor of Gifted Education and Talent Development at the University of Connecticut, where he also serves as the director of the National Research Center on the Gifted and Talented. In March 2000, he was named one of six Board of Trustees Distinguished Professors at the University of Connecticut. He has served on numerous editorial boards in the fields of gifted education, educational psychology and research, and law and education. He also served as a senior research associate for the White House Task Force on Education for the Gifted and Talented. Dr. Renzulli is a fellow in the American Psychological Association and has received distinguished research awards from the National Association for Gifted Children and the University of Connecticut. His major research interests are in identification and programming models for both gifted education and general school improvement.